Akashic U.S. Presidents Series

ADAM HASLETT ON GEORGE WASHINGTON

Akashic U.S. Presidents Series

ADAM HASLETT ON GEORGE WASHINGTON

Rules of Civility

Akashic Books
New York

Akashic Books presents a thought-provoking series of early writings from United States Presidents, starting with George Washington in this volume and moving chronologically forward to John Adams, Thomas Jefferson, and beyond. Each slim book offers an introduction and additional notes by a groundbreaking contemporary writer. This series is unlike any other Presidential commentaries in print, and is characterized by a critical viewpoint that will provide a counterpoint to the more staid analyses that have traditionally accompanied Presidential writings.

First and last pages of George Washington's transcription of the Rules of Civility, *circa 1744:*

Rules of Civility & Decent Behaviour
In Company and Conversation.

1 Every Action done in Company, ought to be with Some Sign of Respect, to those that are Present.

2 When in Company, put not your Hands to any Part of the Body, not usualy Discovered.

3 Shew nothing to your Freind that may affright him.

4 In the Presence of Others Sing not to yourself with a humming Noise, nor Drum with your Fingers or Feet.

5 If You Cough, Sneeze, Sigh, or Yawn, do it not Loud but Privately; and Speak not in your Yawning, but put Your handkerchief or Hand before your face and turn aside.

6 Sleep not when others Speak, Sit not when others stand, Speak not when you Should hold your Peace, walk not on when others Stop.

7 Put not off your Cloths in the presence of Others, nor go out your Chamber half Drest.

8 At Play and at Fire its Good manners to Give Place to the last Commer, and affect not to Speak Louder than Ordinary.

9 Spit not in the Fire, nor Stoop low before it neither Put your Hands into the Flames to warm them, nor Set your Feet upon the Fire especially if there be meat before it.

10 When you Sit down, Keep your Feet firm and Even, without putting one on the other or Crossing them.

11 Shift not yourself in the Sight of others nor Gnaw your nails.

12 Shake not the head, Feet, or Legs rowl not the Eys lift not one eyebrow higher than the other wry not the mouth, and bedew no mans face with your Spittle, by approaching too near him when you Speak.

104 ...belongs to ye Chiefest in Company to unfold his Napkin and Fall to Meat first, But he ought then to Begin in time & to Dispatch wth Dexterity, that ye Slowest may have time allowed him.

105 Be not Angry at Table whatever happens & if you have reason to be so, Shew it not but on a Chearfull Countenance especially if there be Strangers for Good Humour makes one Dish of Meat a Feast.

106 Set not yourself at ye upper of ye Table but if it be your Due or that ye Master of ye house will have it So, Contend not, least you Should Trouble ye Company.

107th If others talk at Table be attentive but talk not with Meat in your Mouth.

108th When you Speak of God or his Attributes, let it be Seriously & wth Reverence. Honour & Obey your Natural Parents altho they be Poor.

109th Let your Recreations be Manfull not Sinfull.

110th Labour to keep alive in your Breast that Little Spark of Celestial fire Called Conscience.

Finis

The statue of George Washington on the cover of this book is the oldest sculpture in the New York City Parks collection and stands in Union Square. It was modeled by Henry Kirke Brown and dedicated in 1865.

Published by Akashic Books
Introduction and annotations ©2004 Adam Haslett

ISBN: 1-888451-60-2
Library of Congress Control Number: 2004106236
Printed in Canada
First printing

Akashic Books
PO Box 1456
New York, NY 10009
Akashic7@aol.com
www.akashicbooks.com

Contents

Introduction

O NE SUMMER A FEW YEARS AGO, on a particularly inebriated afternoon at a house
some friends of mine were looking after
in upstate New York, I came across a small book of
maxims of good behavior purporting to be by
George Washington. The sheer oddity that our
Founding Father had penned lines such as *"Rinse
not your Mouth in the Presence of Others"* (Rule
101) was only compounded by the book's asser-
tion that he had done so at the age of fourteen. To
explain why, at the time, I seriously wondered if
the text were an elaborate joke, I should add that
the house we were staying in was owned by a writer

whose most acclaimed novel was one of the few books I had ever seen with a blurb from Thomas Pynchon. He was a man with a highly developed sense of the absurd; and he had a large, eclectic library. In my altered state that afternoon, it struck me as entirely possible that our absent host had somewhere come across this curious parody of 18th-century manners and chosen to leave it prominently displayed on the top of a stack of books in his sitting room precisely so that ignorant and unsuspecting guests such as myself would come across it and be stricken with the dilemma of whether or not to credit the idea that the leader of one of the most important revolutions in modern history had written the words, "*If you See any filth or thick Spittle put your foot Dexteriously upon it.*"

No sooner did this little volume have me in its grasp than my equally incapacitated friends entered the room and I began reading aloud to them in a tone of wonder. "*Do not Puff up the Cheeks, Loll not out the tongue rub the hands, or beard, thrust out the lips, or bite them or keep the Lips too open or too Close.*" Combining the diction of the King James

Bible with the subject matter of what to do when one coughs or sneezes, the rules seemed to suggest that our adolescent future President had ascended not Mt. Vernon, but some colonial Mt. Sinai, and there, instead of the tablets of Judeo-Christian morality, had been handed a lesson book in table manners. Incredulity reigned among us.

But what if it were authentic? My friends mused on what the broader discovery and dissemination of the book might portend for our understanding of the meaning of the United States as a political entity. Its implications, though unclear, were clearly enormous. A microcosm of intellectual life on the left, our manic conversation burst forth, shone brightly, and dissipated in a hurry.

Our ignorance of course was as complete as it was enjoyable. This was no Pynchonesque sendup of the 18th century. It turned out that any scholar of the founding generation could tell you that our first President, as a teenager, had indeed copied out 110 rules of civility, and that some historians even cited this fact in their explanation of Washington's famous rectitude and formal bearing.

Thus began the minor odyssey that has led Mr. Johnny Temple to ask me to write the introduction to his imprint's reissue of the *Rules of Civility*, the first installment in a series of Presidential B-sides, books on generally (or apparently) non-political topics that have fallen out of public view. While I doubt this service to our nation will garner accolades from our current leaders (in fact, my annotation of these rules will more or less insure that it doesn't), it will hopefully not go unrecognized as part of an effort to better understand the men who have held the highest office in the land, an office which at the beginning of the 21st century has become the greatest agglomeration of military and economic power in human history. In the musings, occasional pieces, and sociological adventures of our leaders, might we discover the basements, cupboards, and antechambers in the mind of power? If so, then it will be well worth the effort. At no time since the height of the Cold War and the anticommunist witch hunts has it been more important for us to understand the pathologies of political authority in this country.

Happily, Washington's *Rules of Civility* provides us with the opportunity not only to gain insight into the 18th-century culture of manners that helped form our first President, but also gives us a set of precepts we might use to evaluate the behavior of our current administration, as I do a bit of in my occasional comments in the text. It is, then, an ideal place to begin this series of lesser known Presidential writings.

WHILE THERE IS DEBATE AND UNCERTAINTY as to how the *Rules of Civility* made their way to Virginia and into the hands of the young Washington, historians agree that whatever version he copied, its point of origin was the *Rules of Civility & Decent Behaviour in Company and Conversation,* a manual composed by French Jesuits in 1595. The first English translation appeared in 1640 and went into several printings over the next forty years. One possibility is that Washington was given an English translation of the rules by a tutor as an exercise in penmanship. Whatever the case, Washington was not the author of the rules, but a copyist.

There are, in my view, two basic categories into which the rules fall. The first contains precepts of general applicability having to do with table manners, comportment during conversation, and the clothing and display of the body. Thus, Rule 14: *"Turn not your Back to others especially in Speaking, Jog not the Table or Desk on which Another reads or writes, lean not upon any one."* The second and often overlapping group contains those rules which are primarily concerned with the etiquette of class. These are aimed at instructing the reader on how to correctly perform their role in the social hierarchy. Thus, Rule 29: *"When you meet with one of Greater Quality than yourself, Stop, and retire especially if it be at a Door or any Straight place to give way for him to Pass"*; and Rule 59: *"Never express anything unbecoming, nor Act against the Rules Moral before your inferiours,"* which contains the perfectly aristocratic and French implication that morality is and always has been something for the lower classes.

Etiquette, of course, has its origin in royal courts and was nowhere more fully elaborated than in the French monarchy of the 17th and 18th centuries. Proper manners, along with proper dress and the right accent, were required for entry into the highest circles. The great ambition of the bourgeoisie from the French fop to the Ralph Lauren shopper was and remains the meticulous aping of the aristocrat.

It makes perfect sense, then, that a child of the gentry should be handed a copy of these rules in the American colonies in the 18th century. Good manners and basic hygiene were often lacking (thus the need to dexterously stamp out that filth), and there was a rising farmer and merchant class seeking political autonomy along with the maintenance of a version of class hierarchy that would act as a bulwark against the direct democracy of the rabble (remember in this regard that Senators were not subject to popular election until well into the 19th century). The *Rules of Civility* take on both concerns, guiding their reader through difficult situations from soup eating—let it cool rather than blowing on it (Rule 94)—to conversing with your betters—submit with modesty to their judgment (Rule 40).

All of which is not to say that the *Rules of Civility* don't contain a lot of good advice. They do. We should be able to maintain a critically minded stance toward the second, class-enforcing category of the rules and their antidemocratic impulse, while realizing that if people followed some of the rules of general applicability the world would be a better place. For one thing, there would be fewer boorish people and boorish conversations. The rules are nowhere more timeless than in their advice on how to talk to your fellow man. Rule 41: "*Undertake not to Teach your equal in the art himself Proffesses; it Savours of arrogancy.*" You bet it does. And it's boring as all get out. Who among us hasn't been lashed to the mast of an interminable conversation consisting of some ignoramus proving his superior knowledge of history to an historian, or bridge building to an engineer? If in such situations we could simply note, quietly, a Rule 41 violation and end it there, how much less dangerous dinner parties would be. And who in the meeting-crazed corporate world wouldn't weep tears of joy at the legislative adoption of Rule 35: "*Let your Discourse with Men of Business be Short and Comprehensive.*" Those struck by illness might be sorely tempted to hoist over their doors a banner bearing Rule 38: "*In visiting the Sick, do not Presently play the Physicion if you be not Knowing therein*"—i.e., please could we not talk about your neck ache on the eve of my back surgery?

Precepts such as these make the *Rules of Civility* both a pleasure to read as well as a resource to guide aspects of contemporary behavior. Alas, as is the case with so many of the writings of our Founders, the neoconservatives have lighted upon this minor text of Washington, and laying their ideological grid down upon it, have discovered— surprise, surprise—yet another reason why the 1960s were a disaster whose influence must be eradicated from the culture.

Let me back up and explain. According to conservative columnist and Washington biographer Richard Brookhiser, the reason the *Rules of Civility* are not taken seriously today is that this country has succumbed to a cult of authenticity, an idea that self-expression, direct experience, and a lack of formality in human relations constitute a kind of natural state against which is set the repressive strictures of traditional society. While Brookhiser correctly identifies the American origins of this idea in Thoreau and Emerson, the modern source of the view is Rousseau and his notion that social life itself, with its inevitable comparisons and envies, casts natural man from the garden of unself-consciousness and ushers him into a world of strife and discord. Hobbes and Locke didn't agree with this speculative history of human development, and nor did our Founding Fathers, who tended to view the state of nature as a place of anarchy and violence, not innocence. While Rousseau and the Romantics that followed him might see many of the *Rules of Civility* as the height of artificial, inauthentic behavior, Brookhiser finds in them the possibility of greatness working its way from the outside in: If we follow the rules, the inner man will be trained by the outer decorum, and the respect for others that the rules encourage will move from the surface of action into the heart of intention. Good manners will lead to great men.

In the neoconservative worldview, the 1960s were the apotheosis of this rude cult of authenticity and as such an entirely regrettable setback for the possibility of future greatness in the American character. Obscured or simply ignored in this account of our recent past is the fact that it was during that same decade that millions of Americans struggled and partially won the right to be treated with basic human dignity, let alone proper etiquette. The Southern tradition of courtly manners, that was no doubt the most faithful to the class dimension of Washington's *Rules of Civility* as compared with any other regional way of life in the country, produced, among other citizens, George Wallace and Bull Connor, who might both have profited from a more expansive reading of Rule 1: "*Every Action done in Company, ought to be with Some Sign of Respect, to those that are Present.*"

I tarry with Brookhiser's comments about the '60s first to point out that manners can flourish in the absence of character and act to hide cruelty, and second to make a small stand against twenty years of neoconservative attempts to co-opt the writings of the Founders into a narrow political agenda that now more boldly than ever seeks to roll back fifty or perhaps even a hundred years of progress toward social and economic justice. One need look no further than Martin Luther King, Jr.'s speech at the Lincoln Memorial to understand the vital importance of fighting for the meaning of our founding documents and their Enlightenment promises against those that seek to read them as little more than a declaration of property rights.

However, I digress. I lose my sense of humor. Living under the second Bush Administration can do that to you. Let us remind ourselves that there is real enjoyment and instruction to be had in these rules, and that readers are encouraged to revel in the grammar and apply the rules far and wide. Particularly active citizens might send our current President a telegram of Rule 73: *"Think before you Speak pronounce not imperfectly nor bring out your Words too hastily but orderly & distinctly."*

Those with an interest in foreign policy and a metaphoric cast of mind might append Rule 97 to their White House missive: *"Put not another bite into your Mouth til the former be Swallowed let not your morsels be too big for the Gowls."*

Finally, we should remind ourselves that Washington's exercise in penmanship stands toward the beginning of a long line of American books of advice to the common man, from Benjamin Franklin's *Poor Richard's Almanac* to the burgeoning self-help sections of your local bookstore. A country bent on self-improvement, personal as well as political, we are ever seeking the way forward and seem happy to grant charlatan after charlatan the status of sage. In this, at least, Washington's *Rules of Civility* have to them a certain gravitas lent them by the future greatness of their adolescent copyist. *"Cleanse not your teeth with the Table Cloth Napkin"* might appear a trivial bit of manners, but to know that it was transcribed and presumably followed by our first President grants it an historical echo missing from, say, *The Rules*, that latter day dating manual with its ukase that one shouldn't play phone messages in the presence of a date lest you lose an aura of mystery when your young quarry hears your mother reminding you that you have run out of mayonnaise. Here, then, is high-brow self-improvement for the funnier angels of our nature. Enjoy and obey.

Adam Haslett
New York City
July 2004

RULES OF CIVILITY & DECENT BEHAVIOUR IN COMPANY AND CONVERSATION

[George Washington's original spellings and punctuation remain intact, other than the numbering, which has been corrected; Adam Haslett's annotations follow select rules in italics.]

1. Every Action done in Company, ought to be with Some Sign of Respect, to those that are Present.

All the rules that follow are more detailed specifications of this first and most general rule of civility.

2. When in Company, put not your Hands to any Part of the Body, not usualy Discovered.

Dear reader, Sit back, relax, and savor these phrases (but try not to touch yourself while you're at it).

3. Shew Nothing to your Freind that may affright him.

One of the real pleasures of the rules is their oracular quality. Just what does this mean? Clearly something important. Perhaps Colin Powell ought to have been more circumspect with his vial of anthrax.

4. In the Presence of Others Sing not to yourself with a humming Noise, nor Drum with your Fingers or Feet.

Speaking of the U.N., Khrushchev's infamous tirade at the Security Council was likely a serious violation of Rule 4. If you can't drum your feet, surely shoes are out too.

5. If You Cough, Sneeze, Sigh, or Yawn, do it not Loud but Privately; and Speak not in your Yawning, but put Your handkercheif or Hand before your face and turn aside.

6. Sleep not when others Speak, Sit not when others stand, Speak not when you Should hold your Peace, walk not on when others Stop.

Nor sleep through the impeachment trial of a President (as several Senators did).

7. Put not off your Cloths in the presence of Others, nor go out your Chamber half Drest.

Needless to say, California had yet to be colonized.

8. At Play and at Fire its Good manners to Give Place to the last Commer, and affect not to Speak Louder than ordinary.

9. Spit not in the Fire, nor Stoop low before it neither Put your Hands into the Flames to warm them, nor Set your Feet upon the Fire especially if there be meat before it.

10. When you Sit down, Keep your Feet firm and Even, without putting one on the other or Crossing them.

Be not a cowboy, yet be not a meterosexual either.

11. Shift not yourself in the Sight of others nor Gnaw your nails.

12. Shake not the head, Feet, or Legs rowl not the Eys lift not one eyebrow higher than the other wry not the mouth, and bedew no mans face with your Spittle, by approaching too near him when you Speak.

As Foucault pointed out, the power over the citizen begins with a disciplining of the body.

13. Kill no Vermin as Fleas, lice ticks &c in the Sight of Others, if you See any filth or thick

Spittle put your foot Dexteriously upon it if it be upon the Cloths of your Companions, Put it off privately, and if it be upon your own Cloths return Thanks to him who puts it off.

Need we say more?

14. Turn not your Back to others especially in Speaking, Jog not the Table or Desk on which Another reads or writes, lean not upon any one.

15. Keep your Nails clean and Short, also your Hands and Teeth Clean yet without Shewing any great Concern for them.

As has been widely reported, the Bush Administration is plagued by an unduly conspicuous concern for dental hygiene, a preoccupation that borders on a danger to national security.

16. Do not Puff up the Cheeks, Loll not out the tongue rub the Hands, or beard, thrust out the lips, or bite them or keep the Lips too open or too Close.

17. Be no Flatterer, neither Play with any that delights not to be Play'd Withal.

"I loathe Kim Jong Il," President Bush said, obeying the first phrase, though no doubt violating the second.

18. Read no Letters, Books, or Papers in Company but when there is a Necessity for the doing of it you must ask leave: come not near the Books or Writings of Another so as to read them unless desired or give your opinion of them unask'd also look not nigh when another is writing a Letter.

Nor monitor the email of thine employees.

19. let your Countenance be pleasant but in Serious Matters Somewhat grave.

Thus, for instance, when discussing lethal attacks on American soldiers one might want to refrain from saying with a smile, as President Bush did, "Bring 'em on."

20. The Gestures of the Body must be Suited to the discourse you are upon.

To which one might add, strut not in your codpiece and pilot's helmet when prematurely declaring the end of hostilities on the deck of an aircraft carrier idled at taxpayer expense for your shameless photo-op.

21. Reproach none for the Infirmaties of Nature, nor Delight to Put them that have in mind thereof.

22. Shew not yourself glad at the Misfortune of another though he were your enemy.

23. When you see a Crime punished, you may be inwardly Pleased; but always shew Pity to the Suffering Offender.

By, say, pardoning a repentant Christian woman rather than having her executed.

24. Do not laugh too loud or too much at any Publick Spectacle.

We'll try.

25. Superfluous Complements and all Affectation of Ceremonie are to be avoided, yet where due they are not to be Neglected.

26. In Pulling off your Hat to Persons of Distinction, as Noblemen, Justices, Churchmen &c make a Reverence, bowing more or less according to the Custom of the Better Bred, and Quality of the Person. Amongst your equals expect not always that they Should begin with you first, but to Pull off the Hat when there is no need is Affectation, in the Manner of Saluting and resaluting in words keep to the most usual Custom.

In the Republican utopia, of course, the market will sort all this out. There's no reason we shouldn't have a return of aristocratic titles—they'd just be bought and sold on the open market, deference enforced by civil fines for violations of other peoples' property interest in their newly purchased Dukedoms.

27. Tis ill manners to bid one more eminent than yourself be covered as well as not to do it to whom it's due Likewise he that makes too much haste to Put on his hat does not well, yet he ought to Put it on at the first, or at most the Second time of being ask'd; now what is herein Spoken, of Qualification in behaviour in Saluting, ought also to be observed in taking of Place, and Sitting down for ceremonies without Bounds is troublesome.

Huh?

28. If any one come to Speak to you while you are Sitting Stand up tho he be your Inferiour, and when you Present Seats let it be to every one according to his Degree.

When seating guests, then, you might say, Halliburton at my right, ExxonMobil at my left, environmentalists under the table where we can kick them.

29. When you meet with one of Greater Quality than yourself, Stop, and retire especially if it be at a Door or any Straight place to give way for him to Pass.

30. In walking the highest Place in most Countrys Seems to be on the right hand therefore Place yourself on the left of him whom you desire to Honour: but if three walk together the middest Place is the most Honourable the wall is usually given to the most worthy if two walk together.

31. If any one far Surpassess others, either in age, Estate, or Merit yet would give Place to a meaner than himself in his own lodging or elsewhere the

one ought not to except it, So he on the other part should not use much earnestness nor offer it above once or twice.

32. To one that is your equal, or not much inferior you are to give the cheif Place in your Lodging and he to who 'tis offered ought at the first to refuse it but at the Second to accept though not without acknowledging his own unworthiness.

33. They that are in Dignity or in office have in all places Preceedency but whilst they are Young they ought to respect those that are their equals in Birth or other Qualitys, though they have no Publick charge.

34. It is good Manners to prefer them to whom

we Speak before ourselves especially if they be above us with whom in no Sort we ought to begin.

35. Let your Discourse with Men of Business be Short and Comprehensive.

May the chino-and-golf-shirt-clad consultants clogging our national airports take heed.

36. Artificers & Persons of low Degree ought not to use many ceremonies to Lords, or Others of high Degree but Respect and highly Honour them, and those of high Degree ought to treat them with affibility & Courtesie, without Arrogancy.

Thus, you should only bust on servants or poor relatives when they get uppity.

37. In Speaking to men of Quality do not lean nor Look them full in the Face, nor approach too near them at lest Keep a full Pace from them.

38. In visiting the Sick, do not Presently play the Physicion if you be not Knowing therein.

Take that medical dictionary elsewhere you paranoid, hypochondriacal freak.

39. In writing or Speaking, give to every Person his due Title According to his Degree & the Custom of the Place.

40. Strive not with your Superiers in argument, but always Submit your Judgment to others with Modesty.

41. Undertake not to Teach your equal in the art himself Proffesses; it Savours of arrogancy.

42. Let thy ceremonies in Courtesie be proper to the Dignity of his place with whom thou conversest for it is absurd to act the same with a Clown and a Prince.

Fair enough, though the rules fail here to give guidance on how to behave when the Prince is a Clown.

43. Do not express Joy before one sick or in pain

for that contrary Passion will aggravate his Misery.

Chuckle not, ye citizens, when the leader of the world's only superpower windpipes a pretzel causing him to pass out in front of an NFL game.

44. When a man does all he can though it Succeeds not well blame not him that did it.

Good advice all around, its obvious correlative being that when a man doesn't do all he could have, blame is appropriate. For some reason, the words "imminent threat" come to mind.

45. Being to advise or reprehend any one, consider whether it ought to be in publick or in Private; presently, or at Some other time in what terms to do it & in reproving Shew no Sign of Cholar but do it with all Sweetness and Mildness.

46. Take all Admonitions thankfully in what Time or Place Soever given but afterwards not being culpable take a Time & Place convenient to let him him know it that gave them.

47. Mock not nor Jest at any thing of Importance break no Jest that are Sharp Biting and if you Deliver any thing witty and Pleasent abstain from Laughing there at yourself.

As the reader can by now tell, I am a flagrant violator of the opening phrase of Rule 47. Dark times require laughter as surely as they require the determination to elect more principled leaders.

48. Wherein wherein you reprove Another be unblameable yourself; for example is more prevalent than Precepts.

49. Use no Reproachfull Language against any one neither Curse nor Revile.

I promise I'll try.

50. Be not hasty to beleive flying Reports to the Disparagement of any.

51. Wear not your Cloths, foul, unript or Dusty but See they be Brush'd once every day at least and take heed that you approach not to any Uncleaness.

52. In your Apparel be Modest and endeavour to accomodate Nature, rather than to procure Admiration keep to the Fashion of your equals Such as are Civil and orderly with respect to Times and Places.

53. Run not in the Streets, neither go too slowly nor with Mouth open go not Shaking yr Arms kick not the earth with yr feet, go not upon the Toes, nor in a Dancing fashion.

Be not a jogger, nor a slacker, nor some demonstrative hippie.
Just walk from A to B and be done with it already.

54. Play not the Peacock, looking every where about you, to See if you be well Deck't, if your Shoes fit well if your Stokings sit neatly, and Cloths handsomely.

55. Eat not in the Streets, nor in the House, out of Season.

56. Associate yourself with Men of good Quality if you Esteem your own Reputation; for 'tis better to be alone than in bad Company.

Remember, Mr. President, you can still fire them all.

57. In walking up and Down in a House, only with One in Company if he be Greater than yourself, at the first give him the Right hand and Stop not till he does and be not the first that turns, and when you do turn let it be with your face towards him, if he be a Man of Great Quality, walk not with him Cheek by Joul but Somewhat behind him; but yet in Such a Manner that he may easily Speak to you.

And if you manage this without a debilitating self-consciousness as to the location of your face, you'll have done better than most.

58. Let your Conversation be without Malice or Envy, for 'tis a Sign of a Tractable and Commendable Nature: And in all Causes of Passion admit Reason to Govern.

59. Never express anything unbecoming, nor Act agst the Rules Moral before your inferiours.

In front of your peers, on the other hand . . .

60. Be not immodest in urging your Freinds to Discover a Secret.

61. Utter not base and frivilous things amongst grave and Learn'd Men nor very Difficult Questians or Subjects, among the Ignorant or

things hard to be believed, Stuff not your Discourse with Sentences amongst your Betters nor Equals.

62. Speak not of doleful Things in a Time of Mirth or at the Table; Speak not of Melancholy Things as Death and Wounds, and if others Mention them Change if you can the Discourse tell not your Dreams, but to your intimate Friend.

63. A Man ought not to value himself of his Atchievements, or rare Qualities of wit; much less of his riches Virtue or Kindred.

This exemplifies perhaps the worthiest theme of the rules: Be humble.

64. Break not a Jest where none take pleasure in mirth Laugh not aloud, nor at all without Occasion, deride no mans Misfortune, tho' there Seem to be Some cause.

65. Speak not injurious Words neither in Jest nor Earnest Scoff at none although they give Occasion.

66. Be not forward but friendly and Courteous; the first to Salute hear and answer & be not Pensive when it's a time to Converse.

67. Detract not from others neither be excessive in Commanding.

68. Go not thither, where you know not, whether you Shall be Welcome or not. Give not Advice without being Ask'd & when desired do it briefly.

. . . World to Rumsfeld . . . Rumsfeld, please come in . . . Can you hear us?

69. If two contend together take not the part of either unconstrained; and be not obstinate in your own Opinion, in Things indiferent be of the Major Side.

70. Reprehend not the imperfections of others for that belongs to Parents Masters and Superiours.

No one ever accused 16th-century Jesuits of being social democrats.

71. Gaze not on the marks or blemishes of Others and ask not how they came. What you may Speak in Secret to your Friend deliver not before others.

72. Speak not in an unknown Tongue in Company but in your own Language and that as those of Quality do and not as the Vulgar; Sublime matters treat Seriously.

73. Think before you Speak pronounce not imperfectly nor bring out your Words too hastily but orderly & distinctly.

A rule the importance of which President Bush has continuously misunderestimated.

74. When Another Speaks be attentive your Self and disturb not the Audience if any hesitate in his Words help him not nor Prompt him without desired, Interrupt him not, nor Answer him till his Speech be ended.

75. In the midst of Discourse ask not of what one treateth but if you Perceive any Stop because of your coming you may well intreat him gently to Proceed: If a Person of Quality comes in while your Conversing it's handsome to Repeat what was said before.

76. While you are talking, Point not with your Finger at him of Whom you Discourse nor Approach too near him to whom you talk especially to his face.

If Robert Caro's biography of LBJ is any indication, the giant Texan was a serial violator of Rule 76.

77. Treat with men at fit Times about Business & Whisper not in the Company of Others.

78. Make no Comparisons and if any of the Company be Commended for any brave act of Vertue, commend not another for the Same.

79. Be not apt to relate News if you know not the truth thereof. In Discoursing of things you Have heard Name not your Author always A Secret Discover not.

When trying to bully the international community into war by scaring them with evidence of a nuclear weapons program, you might want to avoid knowingly using forged documents.

80. Be not Tedious in Discourse or in reading unless you find the Company pleased therewith.

81. Be not Curious to Know the Affairs of Others neither approach those that Speak in Private.

82. undertake not what you cannot Perform but be Carefull to keep your Promise.

When courting eventual federal bankruptcy with the most irresponsible tax and budgetary policy in United States history, you might want to create a few jobs along the way.

83. When you deliver a matter do it without Passion & with Discretion, however mean the Person be you do it too.

84. When your Superiours talk to any Body hearken not neither Speak nor Laugh.

"Pipe down there, George," Dick said, as he resumed outlining the policy.

85. In Company of these of Higher Quality than yourself Speak not til you are ask'd a Question then Stand upright put of your Hat & Answer in few words.

86. In Disputes, be not So Desireous to overcome as not to give Liberty to each one to deliver his Opinion and Submit to the Judgment of the Major Part especially if they are Judges of the Dispute.

87. Let thy carriage be such as becomes a Man Grave Settled and attentive to that which is spoken. Contradict not at every turn what others Say.

88. Be not tedious in Discourse, make not many Digressigns, nor repeat often the Same manner of Discourse.

In speaking to the national press corps, lace not your unresponsive answers with chunks of your stump speech.

89. Speak not Evil of the absent for it is unjust.

90. Being Set at meat Scratch not neither Spit Cough or blow your Nose except there's a Necessity for it.

91. Make no Shew of taking great Delight in your Victuals, Feed not with Greediness; cut your Bread with a Knife, lean not on the Table neither find fault with what you Eat.

92. Take no Salt or cut Bread with your Knife Greasy.

Lest one be tempted.

93. Entertaining any one at table it is decent to present him wt. meat, Undertake not to help others undesired by the Master.

94. If you Soak bread in the Sauce let it be no more than what you put in your Mouth at a time and blow not your broth at Table but Stay till Cools of it Self.

Sound advice for any table. Stop whistling into the minestrone, already.

95. Put not your meat to your Mouth with your Knife in your hand neither Spit forth the Stones of any fruit Pye upon a Dish nor Cast anything under the table.

96. It's unbecoming to Stoop much to ones Meat Keep your Fingers clean & when foul wipe them on a Corner of your Table Napkin.

97. Put not another bit into your Mouth til the former be Swallowed let not your Morsels be too big for the Gowls.

Indeed. You might also try digesting your invasion of one Muslim nation before invading another.

98. Drink not nor talk with your mouth full neither Gaze about you while you are a Drinking.

A ban on gazing about while drinking would presumably bring social life as we know it to an abrupt halt.

99. Drink not too leisurely nor yet too hastily. Before and after Drinking wipe your Lips breath not then or Ever with too Great a Noise, for its uncivil.

100. Cleanse not your teeth with the Table Cloth Napkin Fork or Knife but if Others do it let it be done wt. a Pick Tooth.

Or one could, as the Queen of England does, go a step further. Reportedly, if breaches of table etiquette occur at a royal dinner, the practice is that the Queen herself, followed then by her guests, makes the same mistake in order that the offender never realize his error and feel discomfort.

101. Rince not your Mouth in the Presence of Others.

And yet it is so much fun.

102. It is out of use to call upon the Company often to Eat nor need you Drink to others every Time you Drink.

103. In Company of your Betters be not longer in eating than they are lay not your Arm but only your hand upon the table.

104. It belongs to the Chiefest in Company to unfold his Napkin and fall to Meat first, But he ought then to Begin in time & to Dispatch with Dexterity that the Slowest may have time allowed him.

105. Be not Angry at Table whatever happens & if you have reason to be so, Shew it not but on a Chearfull Countenance especially if there be Strangers for Good Humour makes one Dish of Meat a Feast.

106. Set not yourself at the upper of the Table but if it Be your Due or that the Master of the house will have it So, Contend not, least you Should Trouble the Company.

107. If others talk at Table be attentive but talk not with Meat in your Mouth.

108. When you Speak of God or his Atributes, let it be Seriously & wt. Reverence. Honour & Obey your Natural Parents altho they be Poor.

109. Let your Recreations be Manfull not Sinfull.

This is the only reference in the Rules *to sin, the rest being purely secular and social in their origins.*

110. Labour to keep alive in your Breast that Little Spark of Celestial fire Called Conscience.

Finis

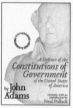
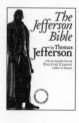